Practical Guide to the Operational Use of the M249 SAW Machine Gun

By Erik Lawrence

Copyright ©2015 Erik Lawrence

I0160089

Erik Lawrence
www.vig-sec.com   erik@vig-sec.com

Although the author and publisher have made every effort to ensure the accuracy and completeness of information contained in this book, we assume no responsibility for the use or misuse of information contained in this book and errors, inaccuracies, omissions, or any inconsistency herein. Portions of this manual are excerpts from outside sources but been validated and modified as necessary.

Printed and bound in the United States of America

First printing 2015

ISBN 13: 978-1-941998-80-9
Ebook ISBN 13: 978-1-941998-81-6

ATTENTION U.S. MILITARY UNITS, U.S. GOVERNMENT AGENCIES, AND PROFESSIONAL ORGANIZATIONS: Quantity discounts are available on bulk purchases of this book. Special books or book excerpts can also be created to fit specific needs. For information, please contact

Erik Lawrence
www.vig-sec.com   erik@vig-sec.com

Firearms are potentially dangerous and must be handled responsibly by individuals. The technical information presented in this manual on the use of the M249 reflects the author's research, beliefs, and experiences. The information in this book is presented for academic study only. Neither the author nor the publisher assumes any responsibility for the use or misuse of information contained in this book.

SAFETY NOTICE
Before starting an inspection, ensure the weapon is cleared. Do not manipulate the trigger until the weapon has been cleared of all ammunition. Inspect the chamber to ensure that it is empty and no ammunition is present. Keep the weapon oriented in a safe direction when loading and handling.

AMMUNITION NOTICE- Firing the incorrect ammunition will damage the weapon and possibly injure the operator.

Training should be received from knowledgeable and experienced operators on this weapons system. Vigilant Security Services, LLC® provides this training and continually perfects its instruction with up-to-date information from actual use.

www.vig-sec.com

Table of Contents

Section 1

MINIMI/M249 Operator Manual Introduction

The objective of this manual is to allow the reader to be able to use the MINIMI/M249 and tripod mount system competently. The manual will give the reader background/specifications of the weapon; instruct on its operation, disassembly, and assembly; demonstrate correct usage of tripod; detail proper firing procedure; and identify malfunction/misfire procedures. Operator-level maintenance will also be detailed to allow the reader to understand fully and become competent in the use and maintenance of the MINIMI/M249 general-purpose machine gun.

Description

General Weapon Specifications
- Mode: Full-automatic only
- Operation: Gas
- Cartridge: 5.56x45mm NATO
- Weight (without tripod or ammunition): 17 lbs./ 7.5 kg
- Overall length: 40.75 inches/1.03 m
- Rate of fire:
    - Sustained   85 rounds per minute (rpm) (with no barrel change)
    - Rapid   200 rpm (with barrel change after two minutes)
    - Cyclic   850 rpm (with barrel change after one minute)

- Range
    - Maximum   3,600 meters
    - Point target   600 meters
    - Area target   800 meters
    - Suppression   1,000 meters

Feed
- Ammunition capacity: 50-round soft nylon box, 100- or 200-round metal box
- Disintegrating metal link M13
- Direction: Left to right
- Basic load is 600 rounds carried in three-200 round boxes

Barrel
- Length: 41 inches/104 cm
- Quick changeable type mechanism
- Muzzle velocity: 3,000 feet per second/915 meters per second

Sights
- Front- protected cylindrical post
- Rear- sight assembly mounts on the top of the cover and feed mechanism assembly.
- The elevation knob drum has range settings from 300 meters to 1,000 meters. Range changes are made on the M249 AR sight by rotating the elevation knob to the desired range setting. Rotation of the rear sight aperture (peep sight) is used for fine changes in elevation or range adjustments, such as during zeroing.
- Each click of the peep sight equals one-half-mil change in elevation, which is .5 cm at 10 meters. The sight adjusts for windage by rotating the windage knob. Each click of windage adjustment also equals a one-half-mil change, which is .5 cm at 10 meters. There is also a windage sliding scale marked with index lines for centering the rear sight aperture.

Action
- Locking feature is a rotary bolt.
- Full automatic from the open bolt
- Safety type is a cross bar push selector with SAFE and FIRE settings.
- Safety location is above the pistol grip.

MINIMI/M249 Background

Figure 1-1 MINIMI Machine Gun

The Minimi is manufactured by Fabrique Nationale in Belgium, while the M249 is made by FNH USA, the American subsidiary of FN. The M249 was the winner of a competition carried out by the U.S. military in the late 1970s–early 1980s for a new squad automatic weapon. The Minimi has been adopted by many other countries since that time, especially among NATO members.

The **M249 Squad Automatic Weapon** (**M249 SAW**) is the United States military designation for a sub-family of the **FN Minimi** squad automatic weapon (from *Mini-mitrailleuse* French: "mini-machine gun." Both are 5.56x45mm NATO light machine guns manufactured by Fabrique Nationale (FN) and its subsidiaries.

The MINIMI/M249 is an air-cooled, gas-operated, fully automatic-only firearm that fires from an open bolt position. It can accept belts of linked 5.56x45 mm NATO (.223 inch) ammunition through the top-mounted feed tray or M16-type magazines through the side-mounted port. The latter allows a SAW gunner to use riflemens' magazines in an emergency if he runs out of belted ammunition, though this often causes jams as the magazine spring cannot adequately keep up with the weapon's high rate of fire. Linked ammunition can be fed from either a loose belt or from a plastic box (or cloth pouch) for 200 rounds, clipped under the receiver. The hard-plastic box has issues with an insecure attachment and by noise producing with movement in its standard form. The M249 SAW features a built-in bipod and a tripod-mounting lug for supported fire, as well as a quick-change barrel that helps prevent overheating during sustained fire. Barrels are engaged and disengaged by rotating the built-in handle, and a spare is normally carried slung in an "A-bag" (accessory bag) by the gunner or his assistant. The forearm is designed to contain a small cleaning kit for field use, though it may not be stored there in practice.

The SAW was developed through Army-led research and development effort and eventually a Joint NDO program in the late 1970s/early 1980s to restore sustained and accurate automatic weapons fire to the fire team and squad. When fielded in the mid-1980s, the SAW was issued as a one-for-one replacement for the designated "automatic rifle" (M16A1) in the Fire Team. In this regard, the SAW filled the void created by the retirement of the Browning Automatic Rifle (BAR) during the 1950s because interim automatic weapons (e.g., M-14E2/M16A1) had failed as viable "base of fire" weapons. Early in the SAW's fielding, the Army identified the need for a Product Improvement Program (PIP) to enhance the weapon. This effort resulted in a "PIP kit" which modifies the barrel, handguard, stock, pistol grip, buffer, and sights.

FN Minimi Variants Designations-

Designation	Nationality	Description
F89	Australia	5.56x45mm NATO FN Minimi machine gun
C9	Canada	5.56x45mm NATO FN Minimi machine gun, steel stock
C9A1	Canada	C9 variant; w/C79 optic
C9A2	Canada	C9 variant; lifetime extension; C8-style retractable stock, accessory mounts, and C79A2 optic
C9	New Zealand	5.56x45mm NATO FN Minimi machine gun, steel stock
Ksp 90	Sweden	5.56x45mm NATO FN Minimi machine gun
Ksp 90 B	Sweden	5.56x45mm NATO FN Minimi machine gun; short barrel, retractable stock, accessory mounts
L108A1	United Kingdom	5.56x45mm NATO FN Minimi machine gun
L110A1	United Kingdom	5.56x45mm NATO FN Minimi Para machine gun
XM249	United States	5.56x45mm FN Minimi machine gun; SAW candidate
XM249E1	United States	XM249 variant; w/1:7-inch rifling
XM249E2/M249	United States	XM249E1 variant; 5.56x45mm NATO FN Minimi machine gun variant w/Product Improvement Program (PIP) kit improvements, including the heat shield
M249E3	United States	5.56x45 mm NATO FN Minimi Para machine gun variant; longer barrel
M249E4	United States	5.56x45mm NATO FN Minimi SPW machine gun; also, incorporating PIP kit improvements
Mk 46 Mod 0	United States	5.56x45mm NATO FN Minimi SPW/M249E4 machine gun variant; fixed buttstock and improved rail handguard

MINIMI

Figure 1-2 MINIMI Machine Gun

The Minimi was the winner of a competition carried out by the U.S. military in the late 1970s–early 1980s for a new squad automatic weapon and was adopted as the US M249, which is made by FNH USA, the American subsidiary of FN. Since then, the Minimi has been adopted by many other countries, especially among NATO members.

The Minimi was one of many firearms that came about, thus NATO's adoption of a new smaller round replacing the previous standard 7.62mm. The winner of the trials was the Belgian cartridge, the SS109, which was developed for use with the Minimi.

The Minimi is manufactured by Fabrique Nationale in Belgium, while the M249 is made by FNH USA, the American subsidiary of FN. The M249 was the winner of a competition carried out by the U.S. military in the late 1970s–early 1980s for a new squad automatic weapon. The Minimi has been adopted by many other countries since that time, especially among NATO members.

M249

Figure 1-3 M249 Machine Gun

The M249 was one of many firearms fielded in the late 1970s, 1980s and 1990s that was part of the NATO adoption of a new smaller round. The Belgian cartridge (SS109), developed for use with the Minimi, was the winner of the competition for the new, standardized 5.56 mm round. In the United States, the M16A2 was adopted following the M249 as part of the move to this compatible, although different, round; firearms intended to fire the SS109 cartridge use a different rifling twist rate (1:7 inches) from the previous U.S. standard M193 5.56 mm cartridge. This weapon weighs 16 pound 8 ounces.

The Minimi and the M249 are not the same weapon — they are different in weight and have slightly different configurations; M249 variants can differ significantly. Although officially adopted in the early 1980s, some early production problems delayed full deployment until the turn of the decade. One thousand Minimis were purchased directly from FN for the Gulf War in 1991, as there were not enough M249s yet in service at the time. The M249 has undergone several variant and improvement programs, though it is scheduled to be replaced by a new lightweight machine gun. In early 2005, a contract for a new light machine gun was issued. The main rival of the Minimi is the Spanish made Ameli, a scaled-down MG3 that takes 5.56mm rounds.

M249 Para Model

Figure 1-4 M249 Para Machine Gun

The compact version of the M249 was designed specifically for airborne operation. A shorter barrel and collapsible buttstock reduce overall length by more than 10" from the standard model. The PARA includes all the standard features of the M249 and can be field-converted to the standard model in just 30 seconds. The M249 Para is a commercial product (law enforcement and military sales only) by FNH USA, not a type classification. It features a metallic, retractable stock and a shorter barrel. It was designed as a paratrooper weapon, although its compact dimensions make it desirable in any combat scenario. The U.S. military did test a short-barreled variant based on a standard M249, but it would appear short-barreled M249s (not M249E4 SPWs or Mk 46 Mod 0s) have been modified to this standard in the field and are not original from factory. The difference between the FN M249 Para and the FN Minimi Para is the use of the so-called PIP (Product Improvement Program) kit developed for the M249, which is also found on all commercial M249 variants. This weapon weighs 15 pounds 15 ounces.

M249E4

The M249-based variant of the FN Minimi Special Purpose Weapon (SPW) has Picatinny rails mounted on the feed cover and handguard, a short barrel, and a Para-style retractable stock. Some features from the SAW and Para models were removed to save weight — these include the STANAG magazine port, the tripod-mounting lug, and the built-in bipod.

Mk 46 Mod 0

Figure 1-5 Mk 46 Mod 0 Machine Gun

Adopted by USSOCOM, the Mk 46 MOD 0 features an improved rail handguard and uses the standard fixed buttstock, which is significantly lighter than the E4's M5 retractable unit from FN. The Mk 46 variant differs notably from the M249 and Minimi in that it is only belt-fed, while the latter work with belts or M16-type magazines. The Mk 46 is lighter due to this change. While extremely similar, the Mk 46 MOD 0 and the M249E4 are not the same weapon. The MK46 MOD 0 is the version of the M249 developed to meet U.S. Special Operations Forces requirements for a lightweight variant that would retain the intrinsic functionality and reliability of the standard model. A major weight reduction was achieved by designing a new, lightweight fluted barrel, removing the carrying handle, magazine well and vehicle mounting lugs. Unique to the MK46 MOD 0 is the M1913 multi-rail system that accommodates scopes, laser designators, and tactical lights. It also has a detachable bipod and includes one spare barrel. This weapon weighs 12 pounds 10 ounces.

CETME Ameli

Figure 1-6 Spanish CETME Ameli Machine Gun

Caliber: 5.56x45mm NATO
Weight: 5.3 kg empty; 6.85 kg with 100 rounds belt in combat box
Length: 900 mm
Length of barrel: 400 mm
Feeding: disintegrating belt, 100 or 200 rounds
Rate of fire: 850-900 or 1200 rounds/min

A Spanish squad automatic weapon which, although aesthetically like a scaled down MG3, has entirely different mechanisms. Internally, it is more akin to the Heckler & Koch HK-21/23 (roller delay), but differs from HK weapons in firing from an open bolt. Very small and light for a belt-fed LMG, it weighs about 2kg less than a Minimi.

The Ameli, externally like the German MG3, is internally much closer to CETME Mod L assault rifle (or Heckler & Koch HK-21 machine gun), having similar roller-delayed blowback action. Some parts are interchangeable between CETME L rifle and Ameli. Ameli is fired from the open bolt. The barrel is quick changeable. The Ameli is fed from disposable plastic boxes that can contain 100 or 200 rounds in belt. The cyclic rate of fire (ROF) can be adjusted with interchangeable bolts, much like the MG3; with the lighter bolt the ROF is about 1200 rounds per minute, and with the heavier bolt, the ROF is about 850-900 rounds per minute.

M249 Ammunition

The SAW forms the basis of firepower for the fire team. The gunner has the option of using 30-round M16 magazines or linked ammunition from pre-loaded 200-round plastic magazines. The gunner's basic load is 600 rounds of linked ammunition.

The 5.56x45mm ammunition used by the M249 is produced by most NATO countries and many other different countries. The 5.56x45mm cartridges will be encountered in both brass and steel cases; however, brass cases are more prolific. The 5.56mm is the diameter of the bullet, 45mm is the length of the case, and it is a rimless cartridge.

Figure 1-7 4:1 ball-to-tracer linked ammunition

The following is a brief list of the different types of ammunition and their uses:

Military Cartridge Types
- **5.56mm, Ball, L2A1** *(United Kingdom)*: 5.56x45mm FN SS109 equivalent produced by Radway Green.

- **5.56mm, Tracer, L1A1** *(United Kingdom)*: 5.56x45mm tracer complement to L2A1, also produced by Radway Green.

- **5.56mm, Ball, M193** *(United States)*: 5.56x45mm 55-grain ball cartridge. Steel core ball -- for use against light material targets, personnel, or training. No tip markings.

- **5.56mm, Tracer, M196** *(United States)*: 5.56x45mm 54-grain tracer cartridge -- for observation of fire, incendiary effects, signaling, and use during training, red cartridge tip.

- **5.56mm, Armor Piercing, M995** *(United States)*: 5.56x45mm 52-grain AP cartridge, black cartridge tip. Armor piercing - for use against lightly armored targets where armor-piercing effects are desired.

- **5.56mm, Ball, M855** *(United States)*: 5.56x45mm 62-grain FN SS109 ball cartridge. Steel core ball - for use against light material targets, personnel, or training. Green tip marking on the bullet.

- **5.56mm, Tracer, M856** *(United States)*: 5.56x45mm 64-grain FN L110 tracer cartridge

- **5.56mm, Blank, M200** *(NATO)* for use during training when simulating live fire. If blanks are to be fired from the MINIMI/M249 machine gun, a blank adapter must first be fitted to the muzzle. Without the blank adapter, insufficient gas pressure is generated to cycle the weapon properly. Crimped purple nose.

MINIMI/M249 Ammunition Containers and Links

The weapon is fed by disintegrating metal link belts. Current belts are joined 25-round sections. Link containers to hold the ammunition belts securely to the bottom of the weapon or onto the tripod include the following.

Based on requests from the field, RFI fielded a 200-round soft pack for the M249 designed to improve weapon retention and reduce the noise signature associated with the standard plastic ammunition container. The program will evaluate all potential candidates and select the 200-round soft pack that meets program requirements. The **M249 200-Round Soft Pack** Program is a follow-on effort to the soft packs provided under the Rapid Fielding Initiative (RFI).

Figure 1-8 200-round soft ammo carriers

Figure 1-9 100-round standard soft ammo carriers

Figure 1-10 200-round standard plastic ammo carrier

Figure 1-11 Can ammunition packaging

Typical packaging is four 200-round plastic boxes in a cotton bandoleer in a sealed metal can with two metal cans in a wooden case for a total of 1600 rounds.

Blank Firing Adapter

The Blank Firing Adapter (BFA) replaces the flash suppressor to allow for the firing of blanks in training exercises. Ensure there is no live ammunition near the event.

Figure 1-12 Blank fire accessories

Installing the blank firing adapter-

1. To install the blank firing adapter, ensure the weapon has been properly cleared.

2. Unscrew the adapter, place on the top of the flash suppressor and tighten down finger tight. If the weapon begins to misfire during use check for tightness.

Section 2

Maintenance

Safety Rules- The following safety rules apply always to all weapons.

1. Treat every weapon as if it were loaded.
2. Never point a weapon at anything you do not intend to shoot.
3. Keep your finger straight and off the trigger until you are ready to fire.
4. Keep the weapon on "SAFE" until you are ready to fire.

Weapons Conditions

Condition 1- Bolt locked to the rear. Safety ON. Ammo on the feed tray. Cover closed.

Condition 2- N/A

Condition 3- Bolt forward. Chamber empty. Safety is off. Ammo on the feed tray. Cover closed.

Condition 4- Bolt forward. Chamber empty. Safety is off. Feed tray is clear of ammo. Cover closed.

Safety

The paramount consideration while training with the machine gun is safety. It is imperative that the weapon be cleared properly before disassembly and inspection.

Clearing the M249 in Condition 1

Weapon Condition 1: An ammunition belt is protruding from the left side; bolt is to the rear and safety on "SAFE."

Figure 2-1 Selector in the "SAFE" position

1. To clear the loaded M249, the weapon's selector must be in the "SAFE" position; push it in to the right side (you will not see the red ring on the crossbar safety) (Figure 2-1).

Figure 2-2 Raising the receiver cover

2. Pinch the feed tray locking buttons and raise the receiver cover to the fully open position. Once the receiver cover is fully opened, remove the ammunition belt link from the feed tray (Figure 2-2).

Figure 2-3 Raising the feed-tray

3. Lift the ammunition feed tray to inspect the chamber to ensure no cartridge is present (Figure 2-3).

Figure 2-4 Closing feed tray and feed tray cover

4. Close the feed tray and the feed-tray cover. Orient the weapon in a safe direction; place weapon on "FIRE" and pull the cocking handle back and ride the bolt forward by the cocking handle. Replace the weapon's selector into the "SAFE" position (Figure 2-4).

Clearing the M249 in Condition 4

Weapon condition 4: No ammunition belt is protruding from the right side.

Figure 2-5 Selector in the "FIRE" position

1. To clear the M249, ensure the weapon's selector is pushed to the left onto "**FIRE**" (Figure 2-5).

Figure 2-6 Pulling the cocking handle to the rear

2. With the right hand (palm up), pull the cocking handle to the rear, ensuring the bolt is locked to the rear and return if forward (Figure 2-6).

Figure 2-7 Selector in the "SAFE" position

3. Place the safety on safe, "**SAFE**" button pushed to the right (Figure 2-7).

Figure 2-8 Raising the receiver cover

4. Raise the receiver cover to the fully open position and observe for live ammunition (Figure 2-8).

Figure 2-9 Raising the feed tray

5. Lift the ammunition feed tray to inspect the chamber to ensure no cartridge is present (Figure 2-9).

Figure 2-10 Riding the bolt forward

6. Close the feed tray and cover assembly, and place the safety to the "FIRE" position. Pull cocking handle to the rear, and pull the trigger while manually riding the bolt forward (Figure 2-10). Close the ejection port cover (Figure 2-11).

Disassembling the M249

To insure the proper function of the M249, it is necessary to disassemble the weapon to inspect and clean the internal components. The names of the parts should be learned through practice in disassembling and reassembling to enhance operator competence. Generally, the parts are named for the functions they perform, i.e., the trigger guard guards the trigger, the cocking handle is used to charge the weapon, etc.

The operator performs general disassembly, which is removing and replacing the eight major groups. Disassembly beyond what is explained in this manual is detailed in the armorer version of this weapon system. During general disassembly, the operator clears the weapon. He ensures the bolt is forward before disassembly, and he places each part on a clean, flat surface, such as a table or mat. This step aids in assembly in reverse order and avoids the loss of parts.

Clear the weapon as per the above description, depending on the weapon's condition.

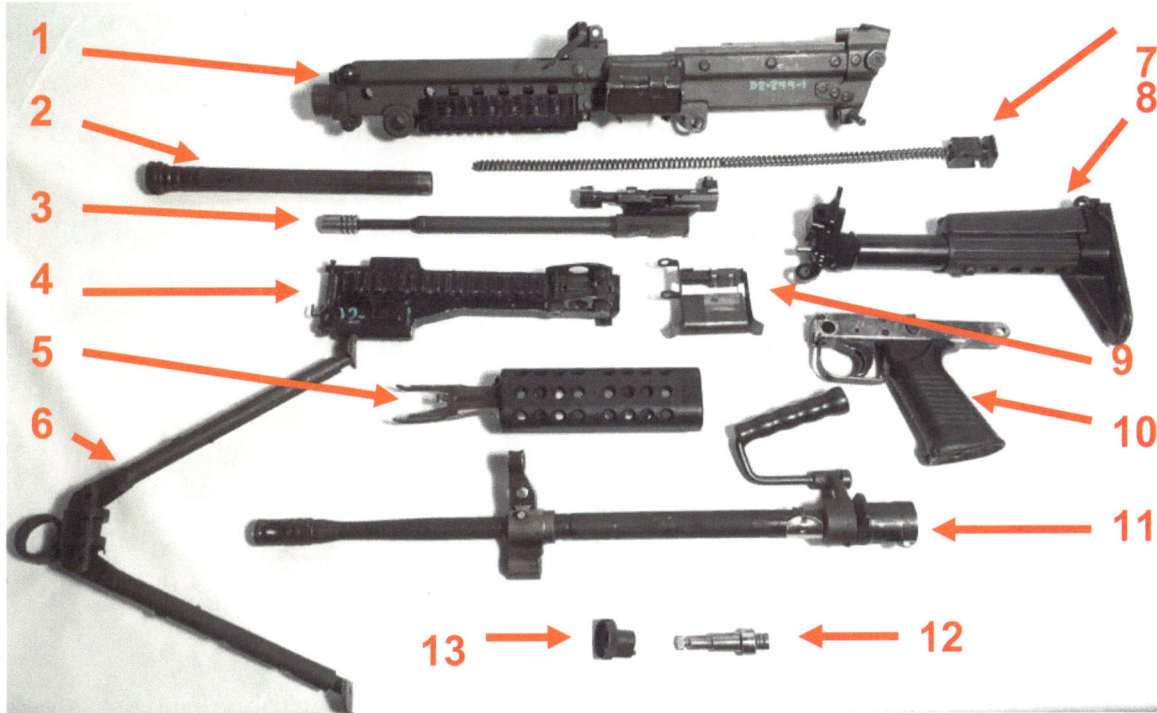

Figure 2-11a Disassembled M249

1 – Receiver
2 – Gas Tube
3 – Bolt Assembly and Piston Rod
4 – Feed Tray Cover
5 – Heat Shield
6 – Bipod
7 – Driving Rod Spring Assembly

8 – Buttstock Assembly
9 – Feed Tray
10 – Trigger Group
11 – Buttstock
12 – Gas Regulator
13 – Gas Regulating Collar

Figure 2-11b M249 Bolt Assembly

When the operator begins to disassemble the weapon, it should be done in the following order:

1. Place the weapon on a flat, clean surface with the muzzle oriented in a safe direction on the extended bipod legs or on the tripod.

Figure 2-12 Rotate the buttstock

2. **Rotate the Buttstock and Remove the Buffer Assembly**- Pull the stock retaining pin to the left. Rotate the buttstock downward on the pivot pin and remove it from the receiver (Figure 2-12).

DANGER- BE SURE THE BOLT IS IN THE FORWARD POSITION BEFORE DISASSEMBLY. THE SPRING GUIDE CAN CAUSE INJURY IF THE OPERATING ROD SPRING IS RETRACTED WITH THE BOLT PULLED TO THE REAR.

Figure 2-13a   **Figure 2-13b**
Removal of driving spring rod assembly

3. **Remove the Driving Spring Rod Assembly**- Push the driving spring rod assembly forward and up to disengage its retaining stud from inside the receiver (Figure 2-13a). Pull rearward on the drive spring rod assembly, removing it from the receiver (Figure 2-13b).

Figure 2-14a   **Figure 2-14b**

Bolt assembly removal

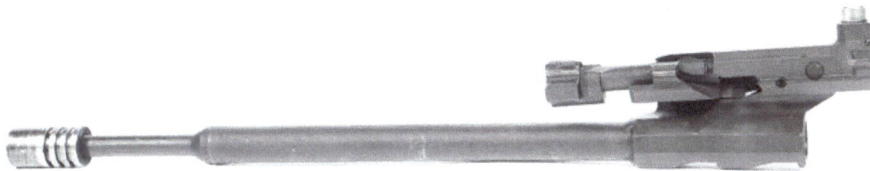

Figure 2-14c Bolt Assembly

4. **Remove the Bolt and Operating Rod Assembly**- Pull the cocking handle to the rear (Figure 2-14a) to start the rearward movement of the bolt and operating rod assembly inside the receiver (Figure 2-14b). With the index finger, reach inside the top of the receiver and push rearward on the face of the bolt until the bolt and operating rod assembly are exposed at the rear of the receiver. Grasp the bolt and operating rod and remove them from the rear of the receiver. Return the cocking handle to the forward position.

NOTE: Pulling the trigger maybe necessary to lower the sear and allow the bolt to release.

WARNING- To avoid injury, keep face away from rear of receiver. Hold rod assembly securely as it is under tension.

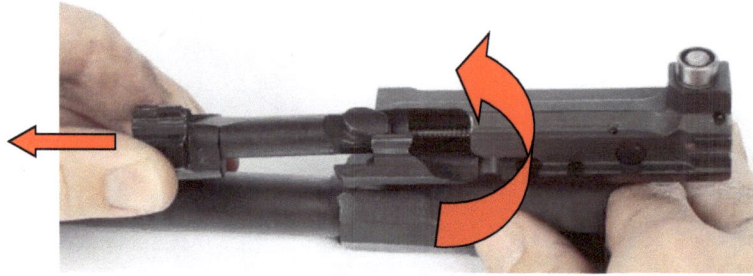

Figure 2-15a

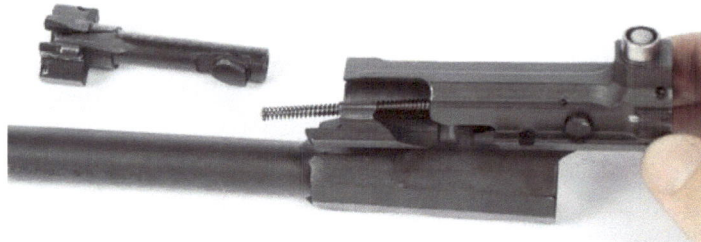

Figure 2-15b
Bolt removal from carrier

5. **Removal of the Bolt from the Bolt Assembly**- Rotate and pull the bolt towards the piston so as the lugs release from the bolt carrier (Figures 2-15a & b).

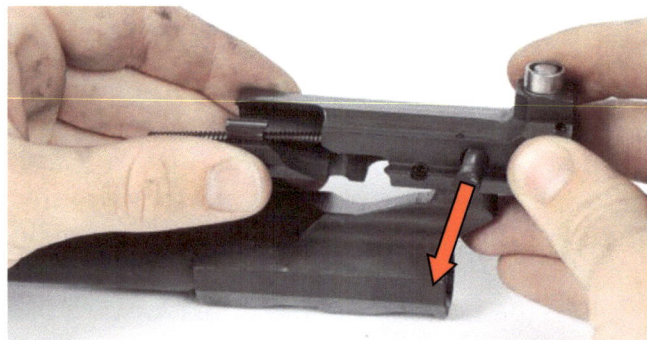

Figure 2-16a

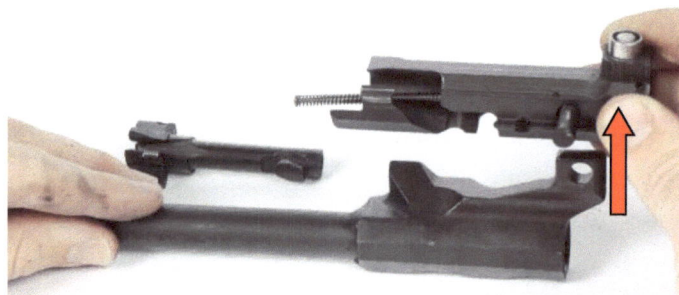

Figure 2-16b
Bolt removal from carrier

Figure 2-16c Disassembled bolt carrier group

6. **Removal of the Bolt Carrier from the Piston Rod**- Push the bolt retaining pin to the left and lift the bolt off the piston rod (Figures 2-16a-c).

Figure 2-17a

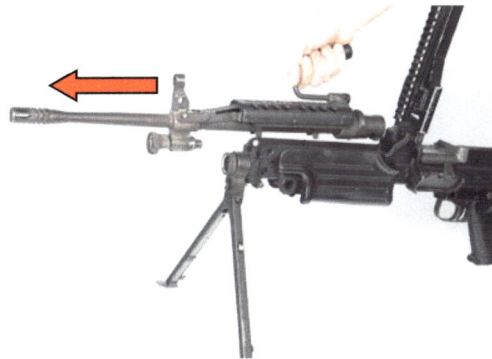

Figure 2-17b

Barrel removal

7. **Remove the Barrel**- Press the barrel release lever to the rear and slide the barrel forward and out of the receiver with the carrying handle (Figures 2-17a & b)

Hold barrel and twist the gas collar left

Figure 2-18a

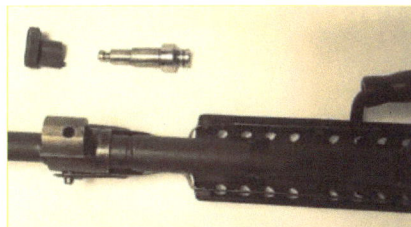

Figure 2-18b
Remove the gas collar and plug

Figure 2-18c Remove the heat shield

Figure 2-18d Disassembled barrel group

8. **Dissemble the Barrel Assembly- NOTE**: some of the newer barrel models do not disassemble. But if they do, then hold the barrel at the point where the gas system attaches to it (Figure 2-18a). Grasp and rotate the gas collar clockwise until it releases from the gas plug. Remove the collar from the gas plug (Figure 2-18b) Slide the gas-regulator plug from front to rear, removing it from the gas-hole bushing. Remove the heat shield. Lift the rear of the heat shield assembly off the barrel; then pry one of the front metal tabs out of the hole on the gas-hole bushing, rotate the heat shield towards the other metal tab, and remove the heat shield from the barrel (Figure 2-18c).

| Figure 2-19a | Figure 2-19b |

Gas tube removal

9. **Remove the Gas Tube**- Rotate the gas tube in front of the bipod while pulling forward to remove it (Figures 2-19a & b).

Figure 2-20a   **Figure 2-20b**
Bipod removal

10. **Remove the Bipod**- Hold the receiver up and pull the bipod attachment ring forward and off (Figures 2-20a & b).

11. **Remove the Forearm**- If the M249 is the older model, you can hold the receiver up and pull the rear of the forearm down and rotate it off. Inside of the forearm should be the cleaning rods and combination tool.

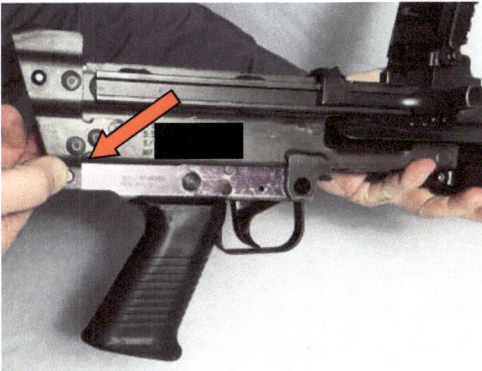
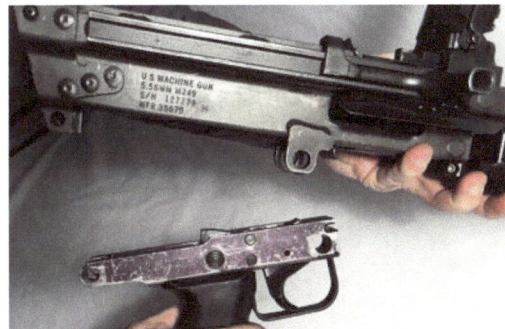

Figure 2-21a   **Figure 2-21b**
Trigger housing retaining pin and housing removal

12. **Remove the Trigger Housing Assembly**- Press the trigger housing retaining pin and pull it to the left (Figure 2-21a). **All pins go from right to left.** Rotate the rear of the trigger-housing group assembly down, disengage the holding notch at the front of the assembly from its recess on the bottom of the receiver, and remove the assembly from the receiver (Figure 2-21b).

WARNING- When buttstock is off, do not pull the cocking handle to the rear without first removing the drive spring assembly.

Figure 2-22a

Figure 2-22b

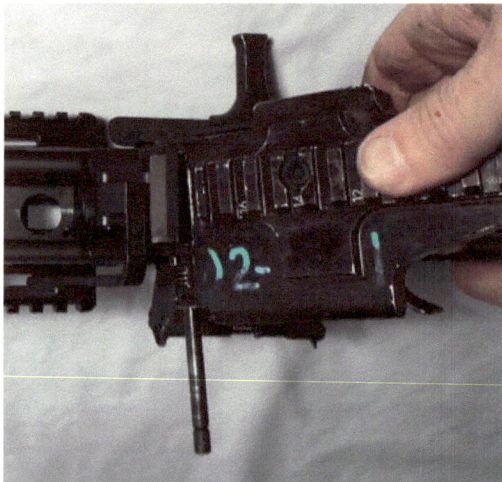
Figure 2-22c

Figure 2-22d

13. **Remove the Cover Assembly**- Close the cover. Rotate the spring pin retainer outward: then push the cover assembly pin to the left (Figure 2-22a & b). **All pins go from right to left**. Depress cover latches, lift upwards, and remove cover assembly (Figure 2-22c). Remove feed tray (Figure 2-22d).

Inspecting the M249

To insure an M249 is serviceable and ready for action, it needs to be inspected periodically and between firings. This inspection can take place while the gun team is cleaning the weapon. Disassemble as per the previous section, and organize the parts in groups to be inspected. Inspection begins with the weapon disassembled into its eight major assemblies. Note that a shiny surface on a part does not mean the parts are unserviceable. The operator inspects each area of the weapon and related equipment for the conditions indicated. Any broken or missing parts should be repaired or replaced. If you see rust on a weapon, the preventive maintenance should be done immediately. Inspect all the components for broken or missing parts. Inspect parts for cracks, dents, burrs, excessive wear, rust, or corrosion. Inspect external surfaces for adequate finish.

1. **Barrel Assembly-** Check barrel for bulges, bends, burrs, and obstructions or pits in the chamber or bore. Disassemble, inspect, and clean the gas collar and plug. Ensure the flash suppressor is fastened securely. Inspect the front sight for damage or looseness. Inspect carrying handle assembly for bent, broken, or missing parts. Ensure the heat shield is present on the barrel assembly, is not bent or broken, and does not have any missing parts.

NOTE: Some heat distortion or charring may be observed on the outer nonmetallic portion of the heat shield and is not cause for replacement. Do not apply lubricants to composite or rubber components.

2. **Buttstock and Buffer Assembly-** Check for burrs and rough edges on mating grooves and flanges. Check to be sure the back-plate latch locks the buffer assembly securely to the receiver assembly when installed. Make sure the buffer plug sticks out through the back plate and is flush or higher than the protrusion below it. Make sure there is no rattling sound when the buffer is shaken and that the plug cannot rotate by finger pressure. Inspect the butt stock for cracks. Check to make sure the back plate locks the butt stock securely to the receiver assembly when installed.

3. **Driving Spring Rod Assembly-** Check the spring for broken strands. Ensure the rod assembly is not bent.

4. **Bolt and Operating Rod Assembly-** Inspect entire area of the bolt and operating rod assembly for missing parts, broken or cracked areas, burrs, bends, or pits on the surface. Looking at the bolt, you can see if the firing pin is broken. The extractor should not move. The operating rod piston should have a slight movement from left to right (about 1/8-inch turn). When the bolt and operating rod are pulled to the rear, the piston should move freely without binding.

NOTE: Always turn both barrels in with the weapon if damage is found on the bolt assembly.

5. **Trigger Mechanism/Housing Assembly**- Inspect the tripping lever and sear for burrs on edges. Push the tripping lever back to raise the sear, put the safety on "S," and pull the trigger. The sear should not drop down far enough to lock in the downward position. Place the safety on "F," and pull the trigger. The sear should drop down and lock in the downward position. Check the sear spring, ensuring the leg of the spring is behind the trigger pin and not between the trigger and the pin. Check grip assembly for loose or missing grip screws. Check trigger guard for bends or cracks. Check trigger spring pin for bends, and/or broken or missing spring.

6. **Cover Assembly**- Pivot the feed lever back and forth to ensure it operates smoothly without binding. Push in on the cover latches to make sure the retaining clip is not weak or missing and that they do not bind in the housing. Push down on the cartridge guides and feed pawls to make sure the springs are not weak or missing. Inspect accessory mounting rail for nicks or burrs.

7. **Feed Tray**- Check for cracks, deformation, broken welds, or loose rivets.

8. **Handguard**- Check handguard for cracks and broken or missing parts.

9. **Receiver Assembly**- Check that the rear sight assembly is securely mounted to the receiver and operates properly. Check that the cocking handle operates the slide properly. Pull the cocking handle to the rear and allow it to return forward slowly, making sure that the slide does not bind in the receiver. Check for damaged or missing ejection port cover, spring, and pin. Lower and raise the bipod legs, ensuring they move freely without binding. Check bipod legs for crack, or twisted or incomplete assembly. Check the exterior surface of the receiver for the exterior protective finish.

M249 completely disassembled and ready for cleaning and inspection

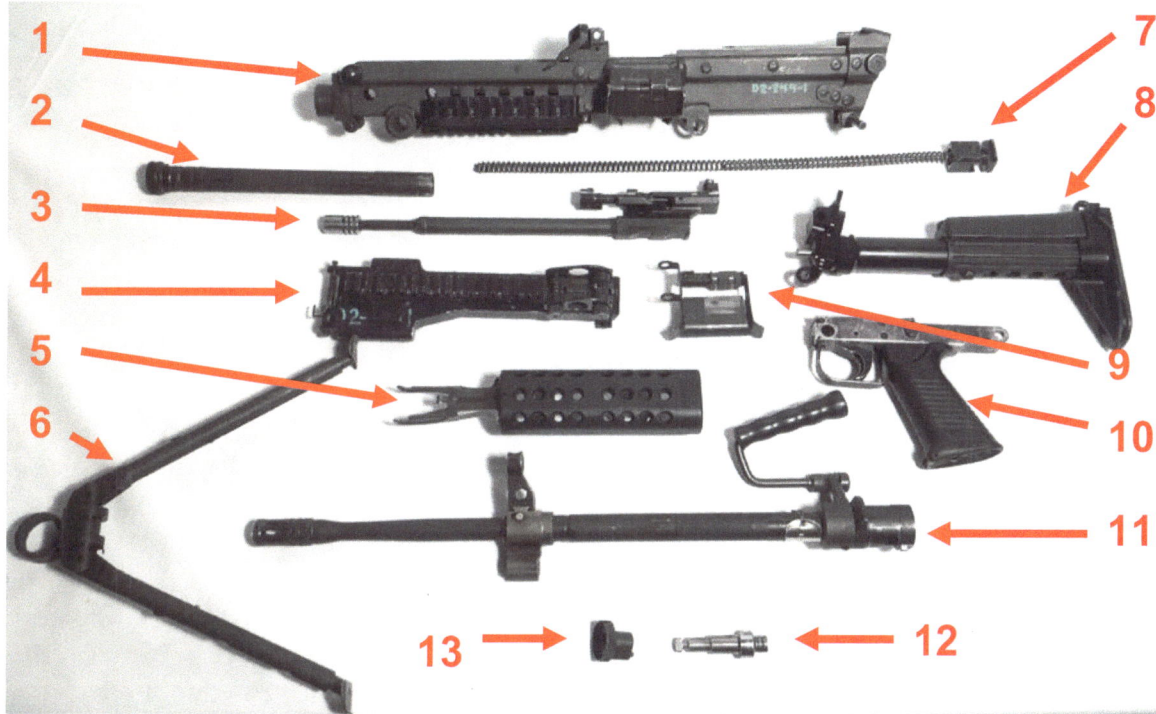

Figure 2-23 Disassembled M249

1 – Receiver
2 – Gas Tube
3 – Bolt Assembly and Piston Rod
4 – Feed Tray Cover
5 – Heat Shield
6 – Bipod
7 – Driving Rod Spring Assembly

8 – Buttstock Assembly
9 – Feed Tray
10 – Trigger Group
11 – Buttstock
12 – Gas Regulator
13 – Gas Regulating Collar

Cleaning, Lubrication and Preventive Maintenance for the M249

The machine gun should be cleaned immediately after firing. At a minimum, the MG should be cleaned after firing a basic load of 900 to 1,200 rounds. The operator disassembles the MG into its major groups for cleaning. All metal components and surfaces that have been exposed to powder fouling should be cleaned using CLP on a bore-cleaning patch. CLP is used on the bristles of the receiver brush to clean the receiver. After the MG is cleaned and wiped dry, a thin coat of CLP is rubbed on with a cloth. This step lubricates and preserves the exposed metal parts during all normal temperature ranges.

CAUTION: When using CLP, do not use other cleaners. Never mix CLP with RBC or LSA. When cleaning the barrel, avoid getting CLP or RBC in the gas regulator. Damage could occur to the weapon.

When cleaning the weapon, any of the previously mentioned cleaning lubricating agents can be used. As soon as possible after firing the M249, the operator disassembles the weapon into its eight major assemblies and cleans them as follows. Before the weapon is disassembled, ensure it is clear.

- Clean the bore using CLP or RBC and a bore brush with a cleaning rod. Do not reverse direction of the bore brush while it is in the bore. Run the brush through the bore several times until most of the powder fouling and other foreign matter has been removed. Swab out the bore several times using a cleaning rod and a swab wet with CLP. Swab out the bore several times using a cleaning rod and a dry swab.
- Clean the chamber using CLP and a chamber brush attached to a cleaning rod. Run the brush through the chamber several times until most of the powder fouling and other foreign matter has been removed. Swab out the chamber several times using a cleaning rod and a swab wet with CLP. Swab out the chamber several times using a cleaning rod and a dry swab.
- Clean the receiver using a receiver brush and CLP. Brush the receiver until most of the powder fouling and other foreign matter is removed. Swab out the receiver several times using a cleaning rod section and a swab wet with CLP. Swab out the receiver several times using a cleaning rod section and a dry swab.
- Clean the gas regulator plug with special tools (cleaning reamers and combination regulator scraper). Remove all carbon dust. Do not use CLP on the collar, gas block, or body. Clean each gas inlet hole of the gas regulator plug. Insert the small reamer into each hole and twist back and forth to remove the carbon (apply hand pressure only). Clean the central hole of the gas plug by inserting the scraper tool down to the bottom of the hole and twisting firmly. Clean the two grooves by inserting the scraper tool into the grooves and applying pressure as firmly as possible.

- Clean the gas cylinder with the special tool scraper-extraction combination tool. Clean the front interior of the gas cylinder by carefully inserting the combination tool, with the handle upward. Be sure the tool is fully inserted and seated against the gas cylinder. Apply slight pressure to the handles and turn clockwise to remove carbon. Clean gas cylinder bore with gas cylinder cleaning brush dampened with CLP. Brush the gas cylinder until most of the powder fouling and other foreign matter are removed.

CAUTION: When inserting the scraper-extractor combination tool into the gas cylinder, ensure before scraping that it is fully seated against the fore-end face of the cylinder. Damage to the fore-end of the gas cylinder could cause gas leakage and subsequent weapon stoppage.

Lubricate the following parts with CLP as instructed:
- Driving spring rod assembly
- Bolt
- Receiver inner walls
- Cover assembly (springs and feed pawls)
- Trigger housing (inside only)

After lubricating, the components are cycled by hand to spread the CLP. Weapons fired infrequently or stored for prolonged periods should have a light film of CLP. This should be applied to the interior of the gas cylinder and the gas piston immediately after cleaning or after inspection. Preventive maintenance is performed every 90 days, unless inspection reveals more frequent servicing is necessary. The use of the lubricant does not eliminate the requirement for cleaning and inspecting to ensure that corrosion has not formed. Before the weapon is used, the gas system and components must be cleaned and free of oil and lubricants.

The following procedures apply to cleaning and lubricating the M249 during unusual conditions:
- Below 0 degrees Fahrenheit - Use lubricating oil, arctic weather (LAW). Oil lightly to avoid freeze-up.
- Extreme heat - Use light coat of CLP.
- Damp or salty air - Use CLP. Clean and apply frequently.
- Sandy or dusty areas - Use CLP. Clean and apply frequently. Wipe with rag after each application to remove excess.

Assembling the M249

While assembling the M249 machine gun, re-inspect the internal parts to ensure that each is in working order. After cleaning, lubricating, and inspecting the weapon, the operator assembles the weapon and performs a function check.

1. **Replacing the Barrel Assembly-** Insert the gas regulator plug into the gas hole bushing. Place the gas collar over the front end of the gas regulator plug; while pushing against the spring, rotate counterclockwise until it stops. Insert one of the metal tabs of the heat shield into the hole located on the sides of the gas hole bushing, and then rotate it so that the other tab locks in place. Then push down on the heat shield so that it snaps onto the barrel. With gas regulator downward and carrying handle in the vertical position, place barrel on the barrel support (located on the gas cylinder). Keeping the gun upright, pull the barrel to the rear, ensuring the gas regulator is guided into the gas cylinder. Pull the barrel fully into the receiver.

2. **Replacing the Cover Assembly and Feed Tray-** Position the feed tray on the receiver so that the feed tray guides are aligned with the receiver brackets. Place the cover assembly onto the receiver, aligning its mounting holes with the mounting brackets on the receiver, and close the cover assembly. Then, insert the spring pin into the holes to affix the cover and feed tray to the receiver (insert the spring of the spring pin into the hole, and then push in from right to left).

3. **Replacing the Trigger Housing Assembly-** Insert the holding notch on the front of the trigger housing into the forward recess on the bottom of the receiver. Rotate the rear of the trigger housing upwards and align the holes of the trigger housing with the mounting bracket on the receiver. Hold the trigger housing assembly and insert the spring pin into the hole, securing the assembly to the receiver.

4. **Replacing the Bolt and Operating Rod Assembly-** Make sure the bolt and operating rod are fully extended (unlocked position). Insert the bolt and operating rod into the rear of the receiver (bolt upward, operating rod beneath bolt), ensuring the bolt is on top of the rails located on the left and right inner walls of the receiver. Push the entire bolt and operating rod assembly into the receiver as far forward as possible. Pull the trigger to allow the sear to drop and the group to slide all the way into the receiver.

5. **Replacing the Driving Spring Rod Assembly-** Insert the driving spring rod assembly into the receiver, sliding it all the way forward against the recess in the rear of the operating rod. Push in and lower the driving spring rod

assembly to engage the retaining stud into the recesses located on the sides of the receiver.

6. **Replacing the Buttstock-** Position the bottom recess grooves of the buttstock onto the top of the receiver recess grooves. Rotate the buttstock up until it stops and then press in the retaining pin.

7. **Replacing the Handguard-** Line up the handguard on the bottom of the gas cylinder, push upwards, and push the cross pin into the guard to lock.

Function Check Procedures

1. Place the safety on "FIRE."

2. Pull the cocking handle to the rear, locking the bolt to the rear of the receiver.

3. Return the cocking handle to the forward position.

4. Place the safety on "SAFE," and close the cover.

5. Pull the trigger (bolt should not go forward).

6. Place the safety on "FIRE."

7. Pull the cocking handle to the rear, pull the trigger, and manually manipulate the bolt several times. Let up on the trigger and pull the bolt to the rear one more time to check that it locks on the sear.

8. Return the bolt to the forward position by holding the cocking handle, pull the trigger, and ride the bolt forward.

Section 3

Operation and Function

The M249 machine gun is loaded from the closed-bolt position. The M249 is fired, unloaded, and cleared from the open-bolt position. The safety must be placed on "FIRE" before the bolt can be pulled to the rear. Before belted ammunition can be used, it must be linked with the double link at the open end of the bandoleer. It must be free of dirt and corrosion. In almost all cases, the M249 machine gun can be best used when fired from a tripod; the M249's potential for continuous, accurate fire and control manipulation is maximized. However, in some circumstances, the operator may use the bipod mount.

Safety Rules- The following safety rules apply always to all weapons.

1. Treat every weapon as if it were loaded.
2. Never point a weapon at anything you do not intend to shoot.
3. Keep your finger straight and off the trigger until you are ready to fire.
4. Keep the weapon on safe until you are ready to fire.

Weapons Conditions

A. Condition 1: Ammunition is in position on the feed tray with the cover closed. The bolt is locked to the rear and the safety is on "**SAFE.**"

B. Condition 2: This weapon condition does not apply to the M249.

C. Condition 3: Ammunition is in position on the feed tray with the cover closed. The chamber is empty. The bolt is forward and the safety is on "**FIRE.**"

D. Condition 4: The feed tray is clear of ammunition, the chamber is empty, the bolt is forward, and the safety is on "**FIRE.**"

Safety

The paramount consideration while training with the machine gun is safety. It is imperative that the weapon be cleared properly before disassembly and inspection.

Clearing the M249 in Condition 1

Weapon Condition 1: An ammunition belt is protruding from the left side; bolt is to the rear and safety on "SAFE."

Figure 3-1 Selector in the "SAFE" position

1. To clear the loaded M249, the weapon's selector must be in the "SAFE" position; push it in to the right side (you will not see the red ring on the crossbar safety) (Figure 3-1).

Figure 3-2 Raising the receiver cover

2. Pinch the feed tray locking buttons and raise the receiver cover to the fully open position. Once the receiver cover is fully opened, remove the ammunition belt link from the feed tray (Figure 3-2).

Figure 3-3 Raising the feed-tray

3. Lift the ammunition feed tray to inspect the chamber to ensure no cartridge is present (Figure 3-3).

Figure 3-4 Closing feed tray and feed tray cover

4. Close the feed tray and the feed-tray cover. Orient the weapon in a safe direction; place weapon on "FIRE" and pull the cocking handle back and ride the bolt forward by the cocking handle. Replace the weapon's selector into the "SAFE" position (Figure 3-4).

Clearing the M249 in Condition 4

Weapon condition 4: No ammunition belt is protruding from the right side.

Figure 3-5 Selector in the "FIRE" position

1. To clear the M249, ensure the weapon's selector is pushed to the left onto **"FIRE"** (Figure 3-5).

Figure 3-6 Pulling the cocking handle to the rear

2. With the right hand (palm up), pull the cocking handle to the rear, ensuring the bolt is locked to the rear and return it forward (Figure 3-6).

Figure 3-7 Selector in the "SAFE" position

3. Place the safety on **"SAFE,"** button pushed to the right (Figure 3-7).

Figure 3-8 Raising the receiver cover

4. Raise the receiver cover to the fully open position and observe for live ammunition (Figure 3-8).

Figure 3-9 Raising the feed tray

5. Lift the ammunition feed tray to inspect the chamber to ensure no cartridge is present (Figure 3-9).

Figure 3-10 Riding the bolt forward

6. Close the feed tray and cover assembly and place the safety to the "FIRE" position. Pull cocking handle to the rear, and pull the trigger while manually riding the bolt forward (Figure 3-10).

Cycle of Function

Operators can recognize and correct stoppages when they know how the M249 machine gun functions. The weapon functions automatically if ammunition is fed into it and the trigger is held to the rear. Each time a round is fired, the parts of the weapon function in a cycle or sequence. Many of the actions occur at the same time. The sequence of functioning is known as the "cycle of functioning."

These actions are separated in this manual only for instructional purposes.

The cycle starts when the first round of the belt is placed in the tray groove. Then the trigger is pulled, releasing the sear from the sear notch. When the trigger is pulled to the rear, the rear of the sear lowers and disengages from the sear notch, allowing the bolt and operating rod assembly to be driven forward by the expansion of the driving spring rod assembly. The cycle stops when the trigger is released and the sear again engages the sear notch on the bolt and operating rod assembly.

The details of the cycle of functioning follows:

(1) *Feeding*. The actuating roller moves the feed lever from side to side, which in turn moves the feed pawls. The forward movement of the bolt forces the outer pawls to the right, fully feeding the round. The inner pawl rides over the round and settles behind it. The rearward movement forces the inner pawl to the right, fully feeding the round. The action of fully feeding a round pushes the link of a fired round out of the side of the gun. The last link in a belt cannot be pushed out and is cleared during unloading.

(2) *Chambering*. The first round is positioned in line with the chamber and is held in position by the cartridge stop and cartridge guide pawl. On trigger squeeze, the nose of the sear is depressed, thus freeing the piston rod extension. The driving spring rod assembly pushes the working parts forward. The feed horn strikes the base of the round. The bolt strips the round from the belt link. The chambering ramp angles downward and, along with the spring tension of the cartridge guide pawl, forces the round toward the chamber. The cartridge guide pawl also holds back the belt link. When the round is fully seated in the chamber, the extractor snaps over the extractor rim of the cartridge, and the ejector is depressed.

WARNING- The M249 is carried loaded with the bolt locked to the *rear* in all *tactical situations* where noise discipline is critical to the success of the mission. Trained gun crews are the only personnel authorized to load the M249 and only when command directs the crew to do so. During *normal training exercises*, the M249 is loaded and carried with the bolt in the *forward position*.

(3) **Locking**. During chambering, as soon as the piston begins to move, the firing pin is withdrawn into the bolt block. The breech remains locked during the primary movement. The bolt enters the barrel breech as the operating rod is driven forward by the drive spring and as the locking lever on which the bolt is riding swings forward, pushing the bolt forward and locking it to the barrel breech. Although the term "locking" is used here, in the M249, the bolt and barrel do not physically interlock. In this configuration, the barrel can be removed when the bolt is forward.

(4) **Firing**. As the working parts come forward and the round is fed into the chamber, the locking lever is forced down by the locking cams. This action slows down the forward movement of the bolt assembly. The piston rod extension, still moving forward, causes the locking lever link to rotate downward and back, forcing the arms down to their fullest extent in front of the locking shoulder. The extractor rises over the base of the round and the ejector is compressed. The round is now fully home with the breech locked. The final forward movement of the piston extension drives the firing pin through the bolt assembly onto the cartridge primer and fires the round. The working parts are now fully forward.

(5) **Unlocking**. When the round is fired, some of the gases pass through the gas plug regulator into the gas cylinder. The rapidly expanding gases enter the hollow end cap of the gas piston and force the operating assembly to the rear, which powers the last four steps in the cycle of functioning. During the primary movement of the operating rod assembly, it moves independently of the bolt for a short distance. At this point, the locking lever begins to swing toward the rear, carrying the bolt with it into its unlocked position, and clearing the barrel breech. When the bolt assembly has been jerked back, slightly enough to unlock the breech, the primary effort is extraction of the empty case.

(6) **Extraction**. When the breech is fully unlocked and the bolt assembly starts its rearward movement, the extractor withdraws the empty case from the chamber.

(7) **Ejecting**. As the cartridge case is withdrawn from the chamber, the ejector pushes from the top, and the extractor pulls from the bottom. The casing falls from the face of the bolt as soon as it reaches the cartridge-ejection port. The empty belt links are forced out the link ejection port as the rearward movement of the bolt causes the next round to be positioned in the tray groove.

(8) **Cocking**. As the working parts continue toward the rear, the return spring is compressed, the trigger stays squeezed, sufficient is gas made available by the gas-regulator adjustment, which causes the working parts to rebound off the buffer, and the action of feeding and firing continues. In releasing the trigger, the sear remains down, but the tripping lever rises. As the working parts come to the rear, the end of the piston rod extension hits the tripping lever, which in turn allows the sear to rise and engage the sear notch, which holds the working parts to the rear.

Loading the M249 Machine Gun

The operator makes sure the weapon is cleared. Place the safety on "FIRE." With your palm facing up, pull the cocking handle to the rear, which puts the bolt assembly in the rear position. When the bolt is held to the rear by the sear, manually return the cocking handle to the forward position and place the safety on "S." Raise the cover assembly and ensure the feed tray, receiver assembly, and chamber are clear. Lower the feed tray, place the safety on "FIRE," and pull the cocking handle to the rear. While maintaining rearward pressure, pull the trigger and ease the bolt assembly forward. Place the first round of the belt in the feed-tray groove, double link leading, with open side of links face down. Hold the belt about six rounds from the loading end while closing the cover assembly. *Ensure that the round remains in the feed tray groove, and close the cover assembly.*

WARNING- The machine gun is carried loaded with the bolt locked to the *rear* in all *tactical situations* where noise discipline is critical to the success of the mission. Trained gun crews are the only personnel authorized to load the MG and only when command directs the crew to do so. During *normal training exercises*, the MG is loaded and carried with the bolt in the *forward position*.

Close the feed tray and cover assembly and place the safety in the "**FIRE**" position. Pull the cocking handle to the rear, and pull the trigger while manually riding the bolt forward. Close the ejection port cover.

Another loading alternative exists when the weapon is not to be used immediately but can be quickly put into action. Have the bolt forward, feed-tray cover closed and locked, and safety selector on "**SAFE.**" Push the exposed double link (brass down) or starter tab until the first round is engaged by the feed pawl.

When you need to load and fire, place the weapon on fire, pull the charging handle to the rear, and return it forward.

Pull the trigger to release the bolt to go forward, repeat the charging sequence, and fire the weapon.

NOTE: This method can also be used as an alternative to opening the feed-tray cover to reload a weapon that has completely fired the belt that was in the weapon. This procedure is how the M2 BMG and Mk 19 are loaded, the double cycle.

Unloading the M249

The operator unloads the M249 by pulling and locking the bolt to the rear position, if it is not already there. Manually return the cocking handle to its forward position. Place the safety on "SAFE." Raise the cover assembly and remove any ammunition or links from the feed tray. Perform the four-point safety check.

Firing the M249

Orient toward the desired area/target, take a proper sight alignment and sight picture, press the safety to the "FIRE" position, and pull the trigger. You would maintain a 6- to 9-round burst for control and avoid overheating the barrel when possible. Firing more than 200 rounds continuously will increase the possibility of cook offs (the heat of the barrel is so great that it ignites the powder in the unchambered round).

Figure 3-11 Selector in "SAFE" position

Once your target engagement is complete, push the safety to the left "SAFE" position. (Figure 3-11).

ENGAGE TARGETS. To engage targets effectively, you will need to know how to employ the gun using the tripod, bipod, and proper body position.

The M249 can be fired utilizing either the attached bipod mount or by mounting the M249 on the tripod. The tripod provides the most stable base for the weapon, enabling the operator to maximize its range capabilities and deliver a high degree of accurate fire on target.

The traversing and elevating (T&E) mechanism permits controlled manipulation in both direction and elevation and makes it possible to engage predetermined targets during darkness or periods of reduced visibility.

Trigger Manipulation

- Pull the trigger to the rear and then release (not squeezed, see the above cycle of function). The weapon can be damaged by not pulling the trigger to the rear quickly and releasing it quickly when firing.

- Bursts of less than 6 rounds should not be fired.

- The rapid rate of fire of 200 rounds per minute is delivered in bursts of 10 to 12 rounds, which are fired 2 to 3 seconds apart.

- The sustained rate of fire of 100 rounds per minute is delivered in bursts of 6 to 9 rounds, which are fired 4 to 5 seconds apart.

- If your sighting bursts impact on the intended target lengthen the burst depending on the effect on target.

MINIMI/M249 Bipod

The M249 and its modernized versions are issued with a folding bipod, which is mounted on the gas tube.

Firing from the Bipod

The rear sight is adjusted to the desired range of target.

Assume a prone position behind the gun with the right shoulder into the weapon.

The right hand grasps the pistol grip and manipulates the trigger.

Place the left hand on the comb of the stock, palm down or up, with the cheek resting lightly against the cover and or the left hand.

Both hands apply a firm steady pressure to the rear during aiming and firing.

The bipod is not stable like a tripod; the body may move.

When changing direction for minor adjustments, shift the shoulders and torso slightly.

When changing direction for major adjustments, the entire body must be moved.

Changing elevation is done by moving the elbows further apart or closer together.

Figure 3-12 M249 Improved Bipod

M249 Improved Bipod leverages the design of the existing bipod and incorporates several features that improve the performance of the M249 weapon. The configuration of the bipod has changed, providing a rugged design that is more durable than the previous version. The result is increased reliability and weapon accuracy. Additionally, the length of the bipod legs can be adjusted to different heights, providing improved stability on uneven terrain.

Figure 3-13 Various M249 collapsible buttstocks

M249 Collapsible Buttstock will allow the weapon to be fired from the shoulder in the extended and collapsed positions, unlike the current product. It maintains a vertical buttstock position for full interface with the operator's shoulder always and provides intermediate, locking firing positions. Weapon control improves when fired in confined spaces such as military operations in urban terrain and air assault operations. Additionally, the buttstock allows ease of ingress/egress from Stryker Brigade Combat Team (SBCT) vehicles and reduces storage space requirements in SBCTs.

Section 4

Performance Problems

Malfunction and Immediate Action Procedures-

A malfunction is a failure of the weapon to function properly. Defective ammunition or improper operation of the weapon by an operator is not considered a malfunction of the weapon. Some of the more common malfunctions of the MINIMI/M249 are sluggish operation and or a runaway weapon.

Sluggish operation and the corrective action - Sluggish operation (gun fires very slowly) of the weapon is usually due to excessive friction caused by dirt or carbon, lack of proper lubrication, burred parts, or excessive loss of gas. On older models, you can move the gas regulator setting to a higher position and re-test until the weapon functions properly. If this step does not correct the sluggish operation, then disassemble, clean, and lubricate the weapon while inspecting the parts for burrs or damage. Replace parts as necessary.

Runaway weapon and corrective action - A runaway weapon is a weapon that continues to fire after the trigger has been released. It may be induced by a worn sear, worn sear notch, or short recoil, i.e., the operating group recoils to feed and fire but not sufficiently enough for the sear to engage the sear notch. Short recoil may be caused by loss of gas or excessive carbon buildup in the operating rod tube. To correct this condition, hold the weapon on target until the ammunition belt is expended or you may kink the belt to stop the feeding of the weapon. Disassemble the weapon and check the gas port plug and gas cylinder extension, and clean the operating rod. Replace parts as necessary and re-test.

Stoppages - A stoppage is an interruption in the cycle of operation caused by a faulty gun or ammunition. In short, the gun stops firing. A stoppage must be cleared quickly by applying immediate action.

Immediate Action - This is the prompt action taken by the gunner to reduce a stoppage of the machine gun without investigating the cause. If the gun stops firing, the gunner performs immediate action. Hang fire and cook off are two terms that describe ammunition condition and should be understood in conjunction with immediate action procedures.

Hang Fire - Occurs when the cartridge primer has detonated after being struck by the firing pin, but some problem with the propellant powder causes it to burn too slowly, and this delays the firing of the projectile. Time (5 seconds) is allotted for this malfunction before investigating a stoppage further because of potential injury to personnel and damage to equipment.

Cook Off - Occurs when the heat of the weapon is high enough to cause the propellant powder inside the round to ignite even though the primer has not been struck. Immediate action is to unload the weapon and allow it cool prior to reloading and firing.

Misfire Procedures

Immediate action - This action is performed when the operator has a failure to fire, which is when the trigger is pulled, the bolt moves forward, and the weapon does not fire. If a cartridge case, belt link, or a round is ejected, push the cocking handle to its forward position, take aim on the target, and pull the trigger. If the weapon does not fire, take remedial action. If a cartridge case, belt link, or a round is not ejected, take remedial action.

Remedial Action - When immediate action fails to reduce the stoppage, remedial action must be taken. Prior to investigating the cause of the stoppage, you must clear the weapon, and this step may involve some disassembly of the weapon and replacement of parts to correct the problem. Remedial actions for stoppages are as follows.

Stuck Cartridge - Some swelling of the cartridge occurs when it fires. If the swelling is excessive, the cartridge will be fixed tightly in the chamber. If the extractor spring has weakened and does not tightly grip the base of the cartridge, it may fail to extract a round when the bolt moves to the rear.

1. Ensure the bolt is locked to the rear.
2. Place the weapon on SAFE and allow the gun to cool if it is a hot gun.
3. Insert a length of cleaning rod into the muzzle to push the round out through the chamber.

WARNING: If nothing is ejected and the barrel is hot (200 rounds or more in 2 minutes or less), do not open the cover. Push the safety to the rear, which places the weapon on safe. Keep the weapon pointed down range and remain clear for 15 minutes, and then clear the weapon.

Ruptured Cartridge - Sometimes a cartridge is in a weakened condition after firing. In addition, it may swell as described above. In this case, a properly functioning extractor may sometimes tear the base of the cartridge off as the bolt moves to the rear, leaving the rest of the cartridge wedged inside the chamber. The ruptured cartridge extractor must be used in this instance to remove it.

Remove the barrel and insert the shell extractor into the chamber to grip and remove the remains of the cartridge.

The ruptured case extractor must be used if the empty cartridge case is ripped in half, leaving the front half of the casing in the chamber and preventing the next loaded round to seat into the chamber. To extract this case neck, you must screw the extractor on the rod section and push it up into the chamber fully so you can pull the case neck out.